What's it Lik

DEMOLITION EXPERT?

Gill Munton

OXFORD

UNIVERSITY PRESS

MW01120797

Contents

Holly Bennett

Holly Bennett is a demolition expert. She is going to tell us about her exciting job.

When did you start this job, Holly?

When I left school, I got a job in an office. I was working for a demolition contractor.

They let me watch a blowdown. It was great! I wanted to have a go myself.

Holly Bennett

- ■ "Demolition" means taking down buildings.
- ■ A "blowdown" is an explosion that knocks a building down.

I joined the blowdown team and started my training. I was 17.

The job can be dangerous. We have to work as a team and trust each other.

Why are buildings blown down?

Some buildings are unsafe. They may fall down and hurt people.

Some buildings are no longer needed. Many tall blocks of flats are blown down because people do not like living in them. Small blocks of flats and houses are built instead.

These flats were built in the 1960s. We blow down lots of flats like these.

Do you wear special clothes?

It can be a dangerous job so I need to wear special clothes.

hard hat

I always have to wear:
- ■ a hard hat
- ■ boots with steel toecaps
- ■ a bright yellow vest.

vest

gloves

boots

I sometimes have to wear:
- ■ big gloves
- ■ goggles over my eyes.

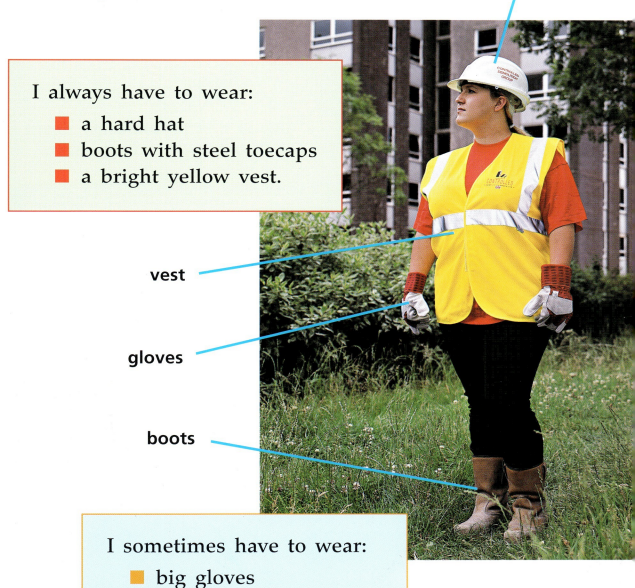

Do you go far to blowdowns?

Buildings are blown down all over the world.
We go all over the UK and to other countries,
such as India and the USA.

I do about 15 blowdowns each year.

This is a hotel we blew down
in Dubai, on the Gulf coast.

What kinds of building do you blow down?

We blow down big buildings, bridges and chimneys.

Before a blowdown, all the traffic is stopped and the roads are closed.

This was the tallest chimney in Europe. It was close to other buildings so we had to make it fall straight, not sideways.

How do you blow down a building?

1 We put a high fence all round the building.
This keeps people away from danger.

DANGER
DEMOLITION
KEEP OUT

We check the
fences every day
to make sure no
one gets in.

 We turn off the gas and electricity.

3 We take out the asbestos.

Workers wear special clothes and masks so they do not come into contact with asbestos.

Inside these cabins, clothes that have been in contact with asbestos are cleaned.

11

4 We look carefully at the building.
We work out:

- which explosives we will need
- where we will put them
- which way the building will fall.

We use plans of the building to help us.

FACT BOX

Explosives are chemicals that burn so fast that they explode.

5 We take out the kitchens, bathrooms, light fittings, floors, windows and doors. This leaves a concrete shell.

These baths were taken out of a block of flats.

The building is left empty.

6 We knock down some of the inside walls.
This makes the building easier to blow down.

We mark the walls that need to come down.

A machine knocks down the walls.

7 We make holes in the walls that are left. This is where the explosives and detonators will go.

ear protectors

mask to keep out the dust

Drilling holes is noisy and makes a lot of dust. Workers must protect their ears and faces.

FACT BOX

A "detonator" is something that sets off an explosion.

8 We wrap parts of the building to stop bits of concrete flying off, because this could be dangerous.

The pillars are wrapped and tied up with rope.

Hay and sand stop bits flying out from under the building.

9 We join up the detonators to the explosives. Then we join the detonators in a long line. This runs out of the building to the firing point.

Explosives are put in holes and fixed with cement.

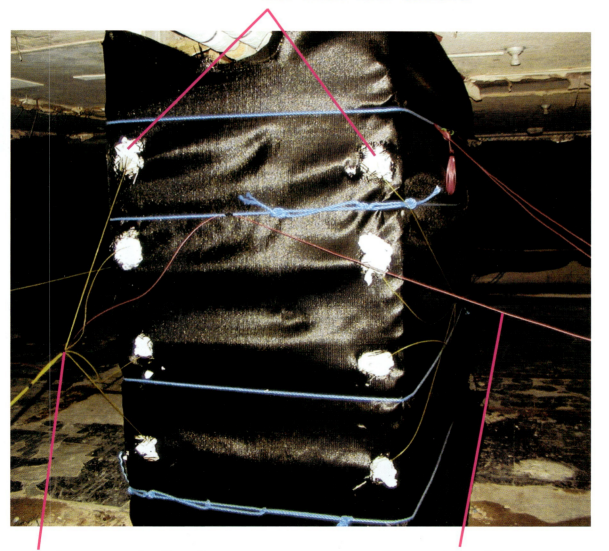

Detonators (yellow) are joined to the explosives.

Connectors (pink) link up the detonators.

10 Everything is ready on demolition day!

- We clear the area.
- We sound a siren.
- We send up a rocket to scare away the birds.
- 10, 9, 8, 7, 6, 5, 4, 3, 2, 1.
- We push the button.

The "button" is usually a handle that is pushed down.

Blowdown!

The building falls down like a pile of toy bricks.

How do you clear up after a blowdown?

A block of flats can leave 5000 to 6000
tonnes of steel and concrete. Some of the
concrete is crushed in a big machine.

A crusher breaks the concrete into smaller
bits. Some bits may be kept on site for
new building work.

Some concrete is taken away in trucks and a lot of it is recycled. It is used to make new roads.

Piles of building rubble can be dangerous. People are kept away until the site is clear.

What is the biggest building you have blown down?

The biggest building was a block of
flats in east London.
It had 22 floors.

Has a blowdown ever gone wrong?

No, because we check everything, then we
check it again – and then we check it again!

What is the worst thing about your job?

I don't like the early mornings! Sometimes we have to get up at 4 a.m.

What is the best thing about your job?

I love to see and hear the blowdown. It is the best feeling in the world!

Index